Lamp Post, My Journey of Finding My Way in the Dark

Cynthia Genesoni

BookLeaf Publishing

India | USA | UK

Presentation by *BookLeaf Publishing*

Web: www.bookleafpub.com

E-mail: info@bookleafpub.com

ISBN: 9789360947934

First edition 2024

To those who I loved and lost, and those who still remain. To my family, and to my friends, old and new, who in the darkness, have helped guide my path with their own light. Thank you all for being my lamp posts.

ACKNOWLEDGEMENT

To my mom, who always believed in me and
told me I was magic.

PREFACE

I hope this book can help you in your healing journey and discover your own inner light within the darkness.

Pulling up a Chair for Grief

When we are met with grief
it visits us and we plead for it to go away
put it in our rearview mirror
back in the distance,
but what would happen if we invited it to stay
and welcomed it
with less resistance?

Perhaps, it would not linger
taking kindly
to our shattered heart,
help us
in not pointing a finger
and
realize that it was destiny
from the start.

So this is my journey
of inviting grief in
to stay
instead of shunning it away
because
through it,
I'll find my way.

The Stoop or the Stairwell

We would playfully disagree
you called it your stoop
when it was clearly a stairwell
over a century old,
covered in gray marble,
worn down by the soles of many travelers
the secrets that these stairs must hold.
Every holiday
I would find you here
sitting peacefully
taking a rest
we would laugh about your stoop
that was clearly a stairwell.
Moments that we shared
would become some of our last.
I don't wait for the holidays
I sit here,
now in your place
it's where I feel you the most
I sit here
peacefully
on your stoop.

Christmas Tree

I wanted nothing to do with you this year.
Why would I?
Why would I want to make space for you?
Tend to you
water you
adorn you with memories
when I know you will just be a constant
reminder
of lost loved ones
no longer here.

As I reassure my heart
that your absence would be better,
grief and joy
both whispered to me.
"I can make room for joy," said grief.
"I will let grief stay," said joy.
I was still not convinced
there was room for both.

The day that I found you,
grief had paid me yet another visit.
The whispers were back
but only from joy.

"I may not always come in big gulps, perhaps,
today,
I can be a small sip."

So I sought you out
brought you home
strung you with lights
decorated you
with both
happy and sad reminders
still
the small sip you were meant to be
could not quench my thirst.
Yet
you stood there, with your branches
strong and proud
as if knowing
I would soon not feel thirsty.
"One last step," said joy.

I turned off the lights
and in that moment
your illumination
reminded me that there can still be light within
the darkness.
That joy and grief
can both dance
harmoniously
within your sparkle.

Thank you Christmas tree
for being the sip I did not know I needed.

Whitney

Sitting here in a cafe in Paris
under a sea of rainbow umbrellas,
I think of how much you would have loved this.
A vision of you was so clear,
cigarette in hand
amongst these handsome men
which I may say,
many were your type.
Then anger hit
because you should be here
celebrating your birthday.
Fuck cancer for ripping that away.

As my joy turned
to sadness,
I felt a pull to go upstairs.
As I made my way
Whitney Houston came on in the emptiness.
For a moment
it was just Whitney and I
wishing we were dancing with somebody
then
for the first time since your soul departed
I saw you
in a mist

but yet so clear.

You were dancing your heart out.
Pure joy
that extinguished
my sadness and anger
because I smiled
knowing
that, in fact, you were there.

Dad

In losing you the day before Thanksgiving
I didn't think you would still be teaching me
things.
But you taught me the biggest lesson in life that
day,
the true meaning of gratitude,
Thank you, Dad,
for I will remember it always.

Samantha

Superstition says
black cats are bad luck.
Oh, my darling, you were anything but that.
In fact,
I believe my life will forever
be sprinkled with good luck
simply because
you were in it.

Addie Mae

The park will always remind me of you,
you would always find the biggest stick
and carry it,
proudly,
for all to see
as we ventured on our journey.

Although it was your backyard for 10 years
you always met it with such a new curiosity
as if
it was your first time discovering it.

Your tail wagging
with such excitement
greeting new
and old friends
along the way,
pure joy,
smiling,
always smiling.

Now I walk it
alone
without you by my side
but

I see you everywhere
and I smile
always smiling.

Songbird

Oh how I miss your singing
the most beautiful sound ever.
When I close my eyes
and sit in silence
I can still hear it
in my heart.
I fear that one day
I will not be able to anymore.
Perhaps, then,
I will look up to the sky
and hear the joy
of your voice
in the angels' choir.

Mother Nature

13

May you heal my heavy heart
as I root down and surrender.
Wrap me in your stillness
so that I may remember.

Inviting Joy In

I am inviting joy in
the way
that I enjoy my whiskey
in small sips
savoring
every last drop.

Running

At a time
when the world seemed
like the flooring under me
was a never ending
sinking hole,
running
gifted me
the solid ground
to steady me.

Writing

I have always found writing
to be healing
for
my hands yearn
to tell the truth
for those
whose mouths
have been bound
by lies.

The Lake

17

I feel like a lake in winter
covered in a bed of snow
that has quickly
turned to ice,
frozen,
waiting to thaw
reminding myself
that underneath
the water waits
patiently
for the heaviness
that lays on top
to melt away
so she can once again
flow freely.

Winter Trees

Spring, summer and fall
have faded away
leaving you bare.
I don't think you get enough recognition
as your sister seasons,
but I think
you are the gentle reminder
that when
everything
is stripped away
under it all
lies the true beauty—
the perfect imperfections
the holes that provide shelter
the essence
the durability
the fierceness
the strength
the majestic
the rebuilding—
many may not see it
but you are the mirror
that reminds us all,
the magic that lies underneath
you unveil

who we are
at our core.

Inner Compass

The woods
are my inner compass,
always
guiding me
back home
to myself.

Lighthouse

I have found refuge
in the darkness
for it has shown me
that I
myself
am the lighthouse.

Self Love

Finding joy
in one's own company
in the midst of solitude
has been a
beautiful discovery
of self love.

My Greatest Teacher

I wonder
when my mother gave me my name,
a name which means Moon Goddess,
it created a spiritual bond
between the moon and I,
where I would always be pulled
towards her
and learn from her.

No matter what phase she is in
she still weaves her magic
waiting patiently
to be full again,
teaching us
that every cycle matters
and they each have a role to play.

I do not need to see her to know she is there
for I can always feel her
trusting
that she is there
and in the darkness
when I need her the most
she always guides me home
reminding me

that
I too,
am the moon.

Mother's Daughter

I remember
that I am
my mother's daughter
but I will not fix my crown,
instead,
I choose to sharpen my sword.

Reflection

My reflection in the mirror
was one
that I was not always comfortable with.
I judged her,
criticized her,
used harsh words on her,
until
one day
I looked long and hard
at the woman staring back at me
and in her eyes
I saw a whole map
a map of my mother
of all the women before me
of all the women I have been
in every lifetime.
Now,
I see a strength
that is carrying me
through this darkness
and I no longer
shy away from her
I say kind words to her
tell her I am proud
I high five

my reflection
For
I find joy
at the woman staring back at me
because
now
I can
finally see her.

Magic in a Bottle

I am
fucking magic in a bottle
I just forgot
to dust myself off.